The Trinity

D0088581

Biblical Truth Simply Explained

Baptism in the Holy Spirit
Jack Hayford

Biblical Meditation
Campbell McAlpine

Blessings and Curses
Derek Prince

Deliverance
Bishop Graham Dow

Forgiveness
John Arnott

The Holy Spirit
Dr. Bob Gordon

Prayer
Joyce Huggett

Rejection
Steve Hepden

Spiritual Protection
Lance Lambert

The Trinity
Jack Hayford

Trust
Tom Marshall

Worship
Jack Hayford

The Trinity

Jack Hayford

Chosen Books

A Division of Baker Book House Co
Grand Rapids, Michigan 49516

© 2001, 2003 by Jack Hayford

Published in the USA in 2003 by Chosen Books
a division of Baker Book House Company
P.O. Box 6287, Grand Rapids, MI 49516-6287
www.bakerbooks.com

Some material previously published by Sovereign World Limited (2001)
and Chosen Books (2003) in *Grounds for Living*

Printed in the United States of America

Library of Congress Cataloging-in-Publication Data
Hayford, Jack W.
    The Trinity / Jack Hayford.
      p. cm. — (Biblical truth simply explained)
    ISBN 0-8007-9350-1
    1. Trinity—Biblical teaching. I. Title. II. Series.

BT112.H34 2003
231'.044—dc21

2003053178

Notes for study leaders

This book is intended to be instructive on all aspects of the Trinity and to help each reader to experience God in all His fullness. Don't be surprised if different opinions and responses arise during the study, particularly when answering certain questions.

As a leader, you will need to balance the needs of individuals with those of the whole group. It is wise to not get sidetracked into devoting too much time to any one person's thoughts, but to enable everyone in the group to share and to respond to the positive message of the book. It will help if the study takes place in an encouraging and receptive atmosphere where group members feel able to share openly.

Encourage group members to read one chapter prior to each meeting and think about the issues in advance. It is usually good to review the content of the particular chapter at the meeting, however, to refresh everyone's memory and to avoid embarrassing those who have not managed to do the "homework."

Five study questions at the end of each chapter are designed to stimulate thought and challenge each person about his or her personal response to God as Father, Son and Holy Spirit. Praying together, asking for God's help, will help you all to take hold of the truths presented.

Our hope is that as readers think and pray through the subject of the Trinity, their personal understanding of God will increase and will cause them to be more fruitful in all areas of their lives. May God bless you as you study this material yourself and lead others in so doing.

Contents

1

Beginning to Know the Trinity

> May the grace of the Lord Jesus Christ, and the love of God, and the fellowship of the Holy Spirit be with you all.
>
> 2 Corinthians 13:14

In the light of God's Word, and the beauty of His self-revelation through creation's glory and redemption's grace, let us begin a study of the eternal Godhead—Father, Son and Holy Spirit. Our theme text from 2 Corinthians is one of many New Testament passages that refer to the Trinity and give evidence of the truth of the persons constituting the Godhead.

We say "persons" because we are forced to use human terminology in our attempt to describe the marvel and mystery of the God above all and the Creator of all. It is clear that they are *three-in-one,* and also that they are entirely *one-in-three.*

Don't be surprised if you find this concept mysterious. It is perfectly logical that the very essence of God's being would exceed our full capacity to understand! Yet God has revealed enough about Himself to show that He welcomes our thoughtful inquiry into this mystery.

The self-revelation of God to humankind has been a progressive unfolding, initiated from His side to ours. If He had not first disclosed Himself, there is no way we could even begin to know or understand Him. But He has revealed Himself and invites us to explore and become open to the wonder of His being.

When the first human was formed and stood upright in the Garden, he immediately met the one who had created him.

God introduced Himself to Adam, gave him instructions on how to live and showed him how his destiny could be fulfilled (Genesis 2:4–20). He clearly assigned to the first couple their role in the Garden (Genesis 1:26–28) and directed them about their relationship with each other (Genesis 2:21–25).

Every aspect of God's heart is unfolded in the story of Eden. He designed a paradise for creatures who have no knowledge of sin or sickness and who are intended for the high destiny and purpose of God. Tragically, through sin these purposes were violated, and the disaster of disobedience removed us all from God's original created order.

Originally, human beings were created with a rich and full revelation of God and an unclouded person-to-person communion with Him. But through the Fall we became blinded to God's glory and goodness. Although Adam and Eve once had clear awareness of God and walked in daily companionship with Him, now, like transmission cables torn by a storm, the lines of contact are down. The world became broken, bound and blinded by sin.

Thank God that in His mercy He set into motion a plan of redemption. This would ultimately bring a Savior to earth who could restore humankind back into relationship with Him and return to them the possibilities intended in His plan for them, personally and collectively.

From the very point of the Fall, God began to restore communications with us. The Scriptures show us how He has tirelessly sought us, so we may know again His grace and salvation. He has mercifully reached into our world, through the ages unfolding to human understanding more and more of His will, His Word and His way. Finally, He has presented us with Himself in His Son, Jesus, God incarnate.

As we walk through the Scriptures, we see a growing revelation of God toward us and His purpose for each person. At every encounter He seeks to reveal more of Himself so that humankind may once more know Him. Knowing God is our primary purpose—to know His heart and His thoughts, to realize His personal interest in us and the economy of His dealings.

The Bible unfolds so much of God's character and love toward human beings that no one should ever need to experience less than a full and intimate relationship with Him. Imagine knowing God's presence in the same way that Adam enjoyed it in the beginning! Yet that is God's objective when He calls us.

To do this we must turn from our own ways and give our lives over to Jesus Christ. In Christ, God has come to redeem every one of us, to purchase us from loss, recondition us with new life and restore us to new hope. Because of Jesus' agonizing death on the cross, fallen humanity can become unchained and once more reestablish an intimate relationship with God.

Knowing the Father through the Lord Jesus Christ requires more than just an initial experience of salvation. It means allowing Him to integrate the life-giving power of the Word into our lives as we allow the Holy Spirit to teach us.

How can we know God?

God wants to reveal Himself to us in ever-increasing ways. He does not wish to remain mysterious or unknowable. He wants us to experience the provision of His strength, grace, goodness and faithfulness. He wants our knowledge of Him to continually deepen.

But to know Him we must come with open, ready, teachable, hungry hearts. Jeremiah 29:13 says, "You will seek me and find me when you seek me with all your heart." This seeking is neither mystically occult nor purely intellectual. To seek with the heart is to commit our will and affections to wanting Him and to open the Word of truth, which teaches us of Him.

Job 11:7–9 says, "Can you fathom the mysteries of God? Can you probe the limits of the Almighty? They are higher than the heavens—what can you do? They are deeper than the depths of the grave—what can you know? Their measure is longer than the earth and wider than the sea."

These words make clear how ill-equipped human beings are to understand God. It is arrogance to think that we can know Him purely by intellectual analysis. We can study the facts about God and grow in mental knowledge, but that is neither what we most need nor what God chiefly wants us to know.

God desires for us to have a heart knowledge of Him, not just a head knowledge. He wants us to know Him, not just know *about* Him. He wants this in order that He might bring to fruition all He intends to do for us and in us.

A mere intellectual pursuit of God is a futile exercise, because His greatness transcends the vain supposition of the most brilliant mind that God could be "learned." This is not to demean human intelligence, but to honestly acknowledge its limits and to follow God's own directives as to how He may be known by us.

Our Creator Father seeks to make Himself known in a way that will allow Him to *apply* that knowledge to our lives. His way is to distill it in a person-to-person way that brings about the change that all of us need in our lives. This is what "knowing" God is all about.

Paul's prayer for the Ephesians

Ephesians 1:17–19 is the apostle Paul's prayer that believers would come to know God: "I keep asking that the God of our Lord Jesus Christ, the glorious Father, may give you the Spirit of wisdom and revelation, so that you may know him better. I pray also that the eyes of your heart may be enlightened in order that you may know the hope to which he has called you, the riches of his glorious inheritance in the saints, and his incomparably great power for us who believe."

His prayer focuses on two specific things:

▶ *"The Spirit of wisdom and revelation"*
Paul was seeking a present work of the Holy Spirit that would impart both wisdom and revelation to the believers. Wisdom refers to specific, practical and workable truth that we receive from God, while revelation is the insight and understanding of how that truth can be applied to lives. This is not vague, superstitious self-delusion. The apostle passionately desired that his people's lives would be increasingly shaped by the knowledge of God.

This New Testament concept of wisdom and revelation is perfectly in line with the thought expressed in Proverbs 1:7: "The fear of the LORD is the beginning of knowledge." It means that fearing God—reverencing Him, understanding His mighty nature and responding to Him appropriately—leads to transformation in our person. When we truly understand God's heart, it inevitably affects the way our lives are lived.

▶ *"That the eyes of your heart may be enlightened in order that you may know the hope to which he has called you"*

Paul wants his people to have more than information. He wants their eyes to be opened to God's calling for them. He desires that the knowledge they are gaining about God may become *incarnate,* that is, in the intimate sense of "knowledge." There must be a practical, penetrating application of God's purposes for us—the "hope to which he has called you."

So we study the character of God so that we might know Him better and respond to Him appropriately. God desires that in knowing Him, we might respond to His purposes for Him. We study doctrine not to accumulate information, but for the practical benefit of our transformation. Doctrinal truth must always be targeted to a practical purpose rather than to philosophical investigation. It's not revealed for us to dabble in or discuss as mere ideology, but so that we might know the way to life and commit to life's way to live.

Study questions:

1. How does the story of the Garden of Eden reveal God's heart for us?
2. What was God's plan of redemption?
3. How can we come to know God?
4. What does Paul pray for the believers at Ephesus so that they might know God better?
5. Is your understanding of God a head knowledge or a heart knowledge?

2

Revelation of the Trinity in Scripture

We now begin to discuss the mystery of the Godhead: the doctrine of the Trinity.

The Trinity, along with the incarnation and eternity, is a great biblical truth. Each one of these concepts is so consummately wonderful that it is incomprehensible to the unaided human mind. They reach into the very nature and being of God Himself, and so they transcend our grasp.

Just as the human mind cannot encompass timelessness (eternity), though we use words or the ideas of physics to attempt it, and just as we cannot compute how the infinite God could confine Himself to finite human form (the incarnation of Christ), though we worship in wonder the birth of our Savior, so it is with the concept of the Trinity. There is no way we can truly apprehend the idea of three persons who are one.

The expansive riches in God's own being exceed the limitations of our human definition of personality. His grandeur shines through our inability to fully define or describe His being. We are humbled by our incapacity to fully assess, analyze or inventory God—He is bigger than life.

God is an entire oneness, complete in Himself ("Hear O Israel: The LORD our God, the LORD is one" [Deuteronomy 6:4]). Yet He is so vast that in the fullness of His very being, He exists as a true "three-ness," overflowing the boundaries of human perception: "I and the Father are one ... And I will ask the Father, and he will give you another Counselor to be with you forever—the Spirit of truth" (John 10:30; 14:16–17).

Although the word *trinity* does not actually appear in the Bible, the concept is clearly present throughout Scripture. Paul in his letter to Titus makes a wonderfully tender statement about the salvation that God has lavished upon us: "But when the kindness and love of God our Savior appeared, he saved us, not because of righteous things we had done, but because of his mercy. He saved us through the washing of rebirth and renewal by the Holy Spirit, whom he poured out on us generously through Jesus Christ our Savior" (Titus 3:4–6).

Notice how the "tri-unity" in the Godhead is referenced. We see the Father ("God our Savior") proactive in a majestic love, sending the Son for our salvation. Jesus Christ is the channel through whom God pours out His abundant love, grace and forgiveness to us. And the Holy Spirit is shown working salvation in us as God extends His cleansing power.

Let us study what God has revealed in both the Old and New Testaments: the three-ness in his oneness.

The Trinity in the Old Testament

From the first moment that we are introduced to God through Scripture, we see that we are dealing with a phenomenon that transcends our intellectual grasp—a multiplicity of personality in the singularity of God. The opening verse of the Bible reads, "In the beginning God created the heavens and the earth" (Genesis 1:1). The Hebrew noun used here—*Elohim*—is plural in form! So from the start God's Word shows us that we are dealing with a plural entity (not entities).

Only verses later, the Scripture reveals that in that plural-singular unity, interaction takes place between what we often refer to as "the members of the Godhead": "Then God said, 'Let us make man in our image, in our likeness'" (Genesis 1:26).

The Hebrew use, here and elsewhere involving God, uses a plural pronoun but the singular form of the verb; and notably, this is God referring to Himself! The plural noun *Elohim* (usually translated "God") almost always occurs throughout the Old Testament as it does in Genesis 1:1—in conjunction with a singular verb: "In the beginning God [plural] created [singular] the heavens and the earth."

Several other texts are offered here where the plural pronoun is used in reference to God:

> And the Lᴏʀᴅ God said, "The man has now become like one of
> us, knowing good and evil."
>
> Genesis 3:22

> The Lᴏʀᴅ said, ... "Come, let us go down and confuse their
> language so they will not understand each other."
>
> Genesis 11:6–7

> Then I heard the voice of the Lord saying, "Whom shall I
> send? And who will go for us?"
>
> Isaiah 6:8

The Shema, Judaism's primary statement of faith, begins
with Deuteronomy 6:4: "Hear, O Israel: The Lᴏʀᴅ our God, the
Lᴏʀᴅ is one." A simplistic translation of the original Hebrew
could read, "Yahweh, God of us, Yahweh is one." But the word
God in this verse is a masculine plural form with a first-person
plural suffix. Because of that, the text could well be translated,
"The Lᴏʀᴅ our Gods, the Lᴏʀᴅ is one"!

So we see a plural reference to God even in this great,
monotheistic statement of Jewish faith. It does not cause any
special conflict to the Jewish people themselves, because they
accept it as an idiosyncrasy of their language. They see it
simply as encompassing the vastness of God and the multiple
aspects of His nature.

Other Old Testament verses, however, do more than merely
hint at the existence of the Trinity through the mysteries of
Hebrew grammar. Here are specific statements that make
reference to the plurality in the essence of God's being:

"Here is my servant, whom I uphold, my chosen one in
whom I delight; I will put my Spirit on him" (Isaiah 42:1; later
quoted in Matthew 12:18). This Scripture clearly distinguishes
three parties involved in the action. The Lord—the Father—is
speaking of the one called "servant"—a reference to the
Messiah—and also of "my Spirit."

A few chapters later we find Isaiah speaking prophetically of
the Messiah's testimony: "And now the Sovereign Lᴏʀᴅ has
sent me, with his Spirit" (Isaiah 48:16). Here we clearly have
the Father ("the Sovereign Lᴏʀᴅ"), the Son ("me") and the

Spirit all in one verse. The distinction drawn between the Lord God and His Spirit and their joint action in sending the Messiah clearly reveal the Trinity.

The Trinity in the New Testament

> As soon as Jesus was baptized, he went up out of the water. At that moment heaven was opened, and he saw the Spirit of God descending like a dove and lighting on him. And a voice from heaven said, "This is my Son, whom I love; with him I am well pleased."
>
> Matthew 3:16–17

The Gospel says that the heavens were "opened" to Jesus. This does not mean that the skies were literally parted, but that the invisible around Him became visible. He saw the Spirit of God descending like a dove and alighting on Him, a miraculous visitation confirming the fact that He was the Messiah. The Holy Spirit was anointing Jesus, fulfilling the literal meaning of *Messiah,* the "Anointed One."

Then the Father spoke from heaven confirming Jesus' identity as His beloved Son. We clearly see the Trinity—each person of the Godhead—in this amazing scene. The Son was being baptized, the Spirit was manifest and the Father was speaking.

Jesus taught the concept of the Trinity in the baptismal formula that He prescribed for us. He commissioned the disciples, "Therefore go and make disciples of all nations, baptizing them in the name of the Father and of the Son and of the Holy Spirit" (Matthew 28:19).

Remember that Jesus was raised in the synagogues as a boy and would have been well acquainted with the affirmation of Deuteronomy 6:4 that "the LORD is one." Yet there is no conflict in His mind regarding the existence of the Trinity. Jesus knew beyond a shadow of a doubt that He had been sent as the representative of the Father, anointed by the power of the Spirit.

Let's consider several other Scripture verses, each of which upholds Trinitarian doctrine. Read through each one carefully; meditate on the truth that is revealed while noticing that each one references the Trinity of God.

The angel answered, "The Holy Spirit will come upon you, and the power of the Most High will overshadow you. So the holy one to be born will be called the Son of God.

Luke 1:35

For the one whom God has sent speaks the words of God, for God gives the Spirit without limit.

John 3:34

You know what has happened throughout Judea, beginning in Galilee after the baptism that John preached—how God anointed Jesus of Nazareth with the Holy Spirit and power, and how he went around doing good and healing all who were under the power of the devil, because God was with him.

Acts 10:37–38

Paul, a servant of Christ Jesus, called to be an apostle and set apart for the gospel of God—the gospel he promised beforehand through his prophets in the Holy Scriptures regarding his Son, who as to his human nature was a descendant of David, and who through the Spirit of holiness was declared with power to be the Son of God by his resurrection from the dead: Jesus Christ our Lord.

Romans 1:1–4

How much more, then, will the blood of Christ, who through the eternal Spirit offered himself unblemished to God, cleanse our consciences from acts that lead to death, so that we may serve the living God!

Hebrews 9:14

Peter, an apostle of Jesus Christ, To God's elect, strangers in the world ... who have been chosen according to the foreknowledge of God the Father, through the sanctifying work of the Spirit, for obedience to Jesus Christ and sprinkling by his blood.

1 Peter 1:1–2

We know that we live in him and he in us, because he has given us of his Spirit. And we have seen and testify that the Father has sent his Son to be the Savior of the world.

1 John 4:13–14

Study questions:

1. Why is the concept of the Trinity incomprehensible to the unaided human mind?
2. How does Hebrew grammar inform us about the nature of the Godhead?
3. In what way is the great Jewish statement of God's oneness also evidence of His plurality?
4. How did Jesus' baptism beautifully testify to the existence of Father, Son and Holy Spirit?
5. Were you aware of how many New Testament verses express Trinitarian truth? Can you find some more?

3

The Value of Understanding the Trinity

God reveals His triune nature to us, and without this self-revelation we would know nothing of the grand reality of His being. It stirs and humbles us. We do not suppose we can master its wonders, nor do we study it simply to store ammunition for arguing with any who deny its truth.

There is intrinsic value in recognizing the three-in-one and one-in-three. Here are two key reasons to study the doctrine of the Trinity:

1. It helps us understand more of God's person (His "personality").
2. It helps us to understand God's work, both in creation and redemption.

It never ceases to amaze me how people consistently attempt to reduce God to a scientifically calculable entity, as if He could be taken into a laboratory and examined. Though we can dissect or expound many texts, we can only conclude that the Bible reveals certain information about God. Yet with our finite minds, we cannot truly grasp the enormity and expansiveness of God.

How can we explain the one through whom all knowledge and wisdom comes? How can we define God, when by His very nature He is beyond definition?

We simply cannot comprehend God or the essence of His being. We are wise to embrace what He has revealed of the facts concerning His immeasurable breadth, depth, length and height, and His timelessness. At best, our faith begins to open to the small glimpses we gain of His grandeur.

The revelation of the Trinity tells us two essential things:

1. *His exceeding greatness is beyond human intelligence and imagination*—and we should expect this. Of course God is beyond our ability to fully define or express. The fact that we cannot totally apprehend His nature does not mean that the concept of the Trinity is incorrect or unreasonable. Rather, it demonstrates that finite minds simply cannot grasp that which is infinite.

2. *Multiple expressions are needed to release the richness and completeness of His Being.* For God to reveal Himself within the limits of the time-space continuum requires human language. It is the only way He can adequately introduce us to the oneness of His person while helping us capture a glimpse of the Father-Son-Spirit in their different functions within the Godhead.

Scripture reveals different operations, administrations and activities of the Father, Son and Holy Spirit. Nevertheless, we cannot limit any person in the Trinity to performing certain tasks. In these various functions of the Godhead, God again surpasses the boundaries of our best understanding, refusing to be contained by the limits of human comprehension.

- The Father may be seen as the Source, the Life Giver and the Creator.
- The Son may be seen as the Substance, the Transmitter, the Communicator, the Messenger and the Word.
- The Spirit may be seen as the Stream, the Life Breath, the Revealer, the Power and the Love of the Father.

Yet in all this, let us humbly remember that whatever the distinct role, action or function we perceive any member of the Godhead to exercise, the Three-in-One are always coequal, coeternal and coexistent in being, power and holiness.

The Trinity helps us to understand creation

The Trinity helps us to understand two primary aspects of God's work—creation and redemption. These are God's major works in regard to all of humankind. The Lord created us, and then due to the fall of humanity, He set into motion a plan of redemption.

Let's look at the action of each member of the Godhead in creation:

- *The Father's will:* The Bible says that all things were created by the Father's will. He determines what will be done and wills that things be (see Genesis 1:1).
- *The Son's word:* While the Father wills, the Son speaks. He declares things, speaking them into existence. The Bible reveals Jesus as the Word who was with God "in the beginning" at the creation of the world so that all things were made through Him (John 1:1–3).
- *The Spirit's work:* The Holy Spirit brings life and power to accomplish the Father's will by the Son's Word. The Holy Spirit is the one who works to accomplish and develop what has already been willed and spoken into being.

The Trinity helps us to understand redemption

Now see how the paradigm revealed in creation was paralleled in redemption as Jesus, the Living Word, stepped into the midst of our fallen humanity.

- *The Father determined:* The Lord always intended goodness, righteousness, blessing and fruitfulness for human beings. He then made it possible for these to be recovered by sending the Son: "For God so loved the world that he gave his one and only Son" (John 3:16).
- *The Son declared:* Jesus spoke and actuated the will of the Father through His life, ministry, death and resurrection. This all became available to the disciples as the Spirit was sent. Titus 3:5–6 says that God "saved us through the washing of rebirth and renewal by the Holy Spirit, whom he poured out on us generously through Jesus Christ our Savior."
- *The Spirit develops:* The Holy Spirit extends the Father's determined will and the declared word of Christ to manifest the full scope of redemption. He convicts us of sin, righteousness and judgment to resurrect us from our

death in trespasses. He births the life of God in us by the power of regeneration, actuating all the power of Calvary. He seeks to develop the character and charisma of Christ (the fruits and gifts of the Spirit) in us.

And that's how we are sent!

What the Father determines, the Son declares and the Holy Spirit develops in you and me. And so the action of the Trinity in creation is reflected in redemption—the new creation.

> For the one whom God has sent speaks the words of God, for God gives the Spirit without limit. The Father loves the Son and has placed everything in his hands. . . .
>   Again Jesus said, "Peace be with you! As the Father has sent me, I am sending you." And with that he breathed on them and said, "Receive the Holy Spirit."
>
> John 3:34–35; 20:21–22

Study questions:

1. Why is it arrogant to suppose that we can comprehend God purely through intellectual study?
2. What does the richness and fullness of God's nature have to do with the Trinity?
3. How have different aspects of the Trinity been expressed in creation?
4. How have different aspects of the Father, Son and Holy Spirit been expressed in redemption?
5. What does this have to do with us today as believers?

4

God the Father

The Trinity at work in human purpose

Just as a study of the Trinity helps to enlarge our understanding of God's person and greatness, it can also help us to more deeply appreciate His individual purposes for us.

In the next three chapters we will focus on the specific roles that the members of the Godhead play in the divine design for each of us:

- the Father, giving us human life and planning a particular purpose for us;
- the Son, rescuing us from sin, giving us spiritual life and recovering us for the Father's original purpose; and
- the Spirit, drawing us to and growing us in Christ, making us functional members of the Body.

We will begin to unveil the richness of God's design in all things. Everything of God's revealed intention relates to His work in both creation and redemption. These point us toward a responsible and meaningful vocation and ministry now, and high destiny eternally.

In this chapter and the following two chapters, we will take a brief overview of the works of the Father, Son and Holy Spirit, with the fullness of God's purposes in mind. In this process we will examine the role that each member of the Godhead plays in the redemption.

Let's look at four aspects of the Father's giving. Each one flows from His grand heart, His wondrous mind and His mighty hand:

He gives human life

God is called "the Father of our spirits" (Hebrews 12:9), acknowledging the fact that our existence flows from His creative activity. He is the one who literally gives breath to our bodies—as Paul said to the Athenians, "He himself gives all life and breath and everything else" (Acts 17:25).

With the creation of the human race, God enabled the capacity to relay human life from generation to generation. In Genesis 2:7, "the LORD God formed a man from the dust of the ground and breathed into his nostrils the breath of life." The Hebrew word for "life" is actually plural.

This does not diminish the reality that each individual person is known to Him and of value to Him. Jesus told the disciples that the ravens neither sow nor reap, yet God feeds them. "And how much more valuable you are than birds!" (Luke 12:24).

He gives us each unique purpose

In Romans 12:3, Paul urges each person, "Think of yourself with sober judgment, in accordance with the measure of faith God has given you." We are to take stock of the investment that God has placed in us—not only our faith, but our unique and distinct motivation. By this I mean the creational gifting that God has placed in each of us, both inclining us and enabling us for our vocations.

John 1:9 speaks of Christ as "the true light that gives light to every man." Lighted by God, human beings can live out and fulfill their created purpose. In Proverbs 20:27 we read, "The lamp of the LORD searches the spirit of a man; it searches out his inmost being."

Because humanity was darkened by sin (2 Corinthians 4:4 says, "The god of this age has blinded the minds of unbelievers, so that they cannot see the light of the gospel of the glory of Christ, who is the image of God"), God's intended purpose for an individual cannot be fully realized apart from saving grace.

Proverbs 24:20 says, "The lamp of the wicked will be snuffed out." The gifts and callings of God lie dormant or function with a self-centered focus while that person lives separate from or in disobedience to Him.

He gave His Son to redeem mankind

> For he has rescued us from the dominion of darkness and brought us into the kingdom of the Son he loves, in whom we have redemption, the forgiveness of sins.
>
> Colossians 1:13–14

Salvation in Christ is the way individuals return to God for forgiveness of sin and for the recovery of their created purpose. Once we are translated from darkness to light, life opens to what Jesus described as life in its fullness, making possible the release of the potential the Father put inside us.

This has always been in the nature of our loving God.

> Who is like the LORD our God,
>   the One who sits enthroned on high,
> who stoops down to look
>   on the heavens and the earth?
> He raises the poor from the dust
>   and lifts the needy from the ash heap;
> he seats them with princes,
>   with the princes of their people.
> He settles the barren woman in her home
>   as the happy mother of children.
>
> Psalm 113:5–9

He gives eternal life to those who receive His Son

Salvation through faith in Christ first reconciles us to our Father Creator: "To all who received him, to those who believed in his name, he gave the right to become children of God—children born not of natural descent, nor of human decision or a husband's will, but born of God" (John 1:12–13).

Secondly, it opens the door to us finding and pursuing our life purpose in God's will.

These graces are ours upon having entered eternal life, which means not only our life beyond this world, but the newness of life that we receive when we are restored to the

Father. It is not only an endless duration of life; it is an expanded dimension of life—both quantity and quality!

John 3:16 tells us that God sent Jesus to die on the cross as an ultimate sacrifice to win back fallen humanity and set us on the road to recovery: "For God so loved the world that he gave his one and only Son, that whoever believes in him shall not perish but have eternal life."

Please understand, to "perish" would mean not only the loss of our eternal souls in eternal judgment, but the loss of the Father's intended purpose for us, in this life as well as eternity. "For the wages of sin is death, but the gift of God is eternal life in Christ Jesus our Lord" (Romans 6:23).

To summarize, every person on earth is a special creation of the Father's human family, endowed by Him with unique purpose and motivation. This is by reason of His workmanship in each one: "For we are God's workmanship, created in Christ Jesus to do good works, which God prepared in advance for us to do" (Ephesians 2:10).

Every person is beloved by Him, even before we understand our sin, our need or our lostness outside Christ. Romans 5:8 tells us that "while we were still sinners, Christ died for us." The Creator hears the cry of every one of His creatures, and He shows mercy to all mankind—even those not yet alive to Him through Christ. "Because of the LORD's great love we are not consumed, for his compassions never fail. They are new every morning; great is your faithfulness" (Lamentations 3:22–23).

However, the purpose of God's mercy is to bring each person to repentance and into a relationship with Him that will last eternally. Paul warned, "Do you show contempt for the riches of his kindness, tolerance and patience, not realizing that God's kindness leads you toward repentance?" (Romans 2:4).

This relationship is available when our new birth in Christ brings us into His redeemed family. Only when we are saved can we "have life, and have it to the full" (John 10:10). This fullness of life restores individuals to the potential fruitfulness we were originally intended for. Not only are our souls saved, but so is His purpose in us!

This is the Father at work in creation and redemption. He gave us life and the incredible promise of treasure in what

He made us to be. Though we lost that due to our sin, He then sent His Son in order to retrieve that treasure. The moment we receive Him, He gives us the quality of life that transforms us now and gives us the hope of being with Him forever, in eternity.

Study questions:

1. How does studying the Trinity help us to understand and take hold of God's purposes for our lives?
2. What do God's gifts of life and His unique plans for each of us tell us about His nature?
3. What part did the Father play in the coming of Jesus to save us?
4. How must we respond to the gift of Christ on the cross in order to be reconciled with the Father?
5. Do you know God as a good giver? Explain.

5

God the Son:
God Revealed in Human Form

Jesus was sent to rescue us from loss and bring fulfillment of all that we were made to be. "For we are God's workmanship, created in Christ Jesus to do good works, which God prepared in advance for us to do" (Ephesians 2:10). Our objective is to help each person grasp more of an insight into God's heart for each one. Dear friends, God sent Jesus not only to save us from our sin, but also to redeem and recover His treasured purpose in us. The horror of sin is not merely its shame and guilt, but also the marring of the divine design.

In the coming of Christ, the whole Godhead was operating more than just a rescue plan. Within the creation of each person, there was a heavenly master plan to destroy sin and recover grace. Salvation means that we can finally hope to realize the original intentions of God.

John's Gospel records one of the most important statements in the entire New Testament. Thomas asked Jesus, "Lord, we don't know where you are going, so how can we know the way?" Jesus answered, "I am the way and the truth and the life. No one comes to the Father except through me" (John 14:5–6).

Our familiarity with the message of saving grace in these words may cause us to overlook a profoundly significant aspect of their meaning. Jesus was expressing His *oneness* with the Father. Not only was He showing the way to the Father, but He was also indicating that the essence of the Father's heart was being shown in His human Son.

Jesus continued, "If you really knew me, you would know my Father as well. From now on, you do know him and have seen him" (John 14:7). When Philip responded by requesting,

"Show us the Father," Jesus' reply was in the past tense, as though to say, "You've seen him already!"—"Anyone who has seen me has seen the Father. How can you say, 'Show us the Father'?" (John 14:9).

Jesus wanted His disciples to grasp the fact that, for the whole time they had been together, He had lived in an unbroken, perfect link with Father God because of His own unique relationship as Son. Jesus had never spoken from His own authority but only as a direct expression of the Father's will, and He consistently affirmed that His works were not His, but the Father's (John 9:4; 10:37–38; 14:10). As God the Son incarnate on earth, He was doing the will and work of God the Father in heaven.

Jesus' words are even more pointed in John 10:30, where he says explicitly, "I and the Father are one." This provides a gateway into our exploration of how Jesus embodies the different names of God. All the attributes of the Father are reflected and demonstrated in the person and ministry of Christ.

When we see the character of Jesus precisely mirroring that of the Father in both nature and quality, it verifies His identity as the Son. We can rejoice in this and receive the promise of these qualities for our own personal needs and circumstances, and draw on the grace that the Savior wants to give us. As we welcome the Lord, these attributes may flow into our own nature by the Holy Spirit, and may grow in us.

> In the beginning was the Word, and the Word was with God, and the Word was God. He was with God in the beginning. Through him all things were made; without him nothing was made that has been made....
> The Word became flesh and made his dwelling among us. We have seen his glory, the glory of the One and Only, who came from the Father, full of grace and truth.
>
> John 1:1–3, 14

We can see clearly that the Bible equates the glory of Jesus, the Son, with that of God the Father. Because Jesus is God, in becoming flesh He manifested the qualities of God revealed in the Old Testament. He was the direct, human expression of God.

Let us give praise to our blessed Savior!

> He is the image of the invisible God, the firstborn over all creation. For by him all things were created: things in heaven and on earth . . . all things were created by him and for him. . . .
> For in Christ all the fullness of the Deity lives in bodily form, and you have been given fullness in Christ.
> Colossians 1:15–16; 2:9–10

Now, look at what the Son of God has given us.

The Son gave His life of His own accord

The Bible tells us that God gave His Son, but then it also shows us that the Son willingly gave His life: "The reason my Father loves me is that I lay down my life—only to take it up again. No one takes it from me, but I lay it down of my own accord. I have authority to lay it down and authority to take it up again. This command I received from my Father" (John 10:17–18).

Later in John's Gospel, on the day of the crucifixion, Pilate urged Jesus to speak up for himself. Pilate claimed power over Jesus' life, but Jesus answered, "You would have no power over me if it were not given to you from above" (John 19:11).

Although as Rome's representative Pilate could sentence Jesus to death, he could neither control God nor conclude Jesus' life unless Jesus willingly yielded it up Himself. Completing His work of redemption on the cross, Jesus called out to the Father: "Father, into your hands I commit my spirit" (Luke 23:46). Only then did He breathe His last.

The Son defeated death

The Scriptures indicate that Jesus, upon surrendering His life at Calvary, descended into hell—*Sheol*, the underworld, "Abraham's bosom," the abode of the dead. 1 Peter 3:18–20 tells us, "He was put to death in the body but made alive in the Spirit, through whom also he went and preached to the spirits in prison who disobeyed long ago when God waited patiently in the days of Noah while the ark was being built."

In Ephesians 4:9, Paul puts it that the Lord "descended to the lower, earthly regions." Jesus did not make this descent in order to suffer further on our behalf. Rather, as He preached to the spirits in prison, He proclaimed the worthiness of the faith that had long anticipated the coming Redeemer and the justice of the judgment on all who had rejected the truth of God.

The resurrection showed that Jesus had truly defeated death. He rose from the dead, never to die again, and then ascended to the Father's right hand to make additional gifts.

The Son pours out the gift of the Holy Spirit

Before His crucifixion, Jesus told His disciples that He would send the Comforter—the Holy Spirit. Then, after His resurrection, He commanded them to stay in Jerusalem until they had been "clothed with power from on high" (Luke 24:49). "Wait for the gift my Father promised, which you have heard me speak about. For John baptized with water, but in a few days you will be baptized with the Holy Spirit" (Acts 1:4–5).

On the day of Pentecost, a supernatural visitation took place that Peter explained to the inquiring crowd, as a multinational group heard the disciples miraculously praising God in languages they had never known. He declared, "God has raised this Jesus to life, and we are all witnesses of the fact. Exalted to the right hand of God, he has received from the Father the promised Holy Spirit and has poured out what you now see and hear" (Acts 2:32–33).

In pouring out the Holy Spirit on His Church, Jesus was unleashing the power for His people to continue to do all that He "began to do and to teach until the day he was taken up to heaven" (Acts 1:1–2).

As we, His people today, learn to grow in full obedience to God, we can increasingly move in the life and power of the Spirit. No longer confined to the physical limits of His human body, now Christ is incarnating Himself in His whole Church by the power of the Spirit.

The Son builds His Church

Having poured out the Spirit, Jesus knows that His people need to be led, fed and cared for, so He passes on His ministry to the Church. To nurture and edify His people He gives "some to be apostles, some to be prophets, some to be evangelists, and some to be pastors and teachers, to prepare God's people for works of service, so that the body of Christ may be built up until we all reach unity in the faith and in the knowledge of the Son of God and become mature, attaining to the whole measure of the fullness of Christ" (Ephesians 4:11–13).

These gifts to the Church are people who will occupy various "servant roles," their essential mission being to assist Christ's people to wholeness, to cultivate them in the Word and to equip them for ministry.

Those with offices of ministry are to be respected and honored for the calling and authority with which Christ has endowed them. But they are called to lay down their lives for the sheep, not "lording it over those entrusted to you, but being examples to the flock" (1 Peter 5:3). While they are to be lovingly and faithfully funded by the body (1 Timothy 5:18), they are not to exploit their positions for personal or financial advantage (1 Peter 5:2).

Leaders must manifest the character of Christ, to develop His life in His people toward the advance of their effectiveness in touching the world in Jesus' name.

In summary, Jesus gave up His life for us, to redeem us and restore us to the Father. Having achieved this "saving work," He set in motion the building of His Church (Matthew 16:13–19). To achieve this He poured out the gift of the Holy Spirit on the Church at its very outset, and He still calls each of His own to be open to the same experience of baptism in the Spirit.

Jesus' life flowing into and through His Church is advanced by people gifted and assigned by Him to help build and shape the people of God. These ministries assist growth, helping believers to recover the creative purpose of the Father put in them from birth. They also equip the Church, in the Word and by the Holy Spirit, to learn to function in faith, faithfulness and power as members of Christ's Body.

Study questions:

1. What is the "heavenly master plan" within creation and salvation for us?

2. How does the oneness of Jesus and the Father make it possible for the "divine design" to be restored in us?
3. How did Jesus' character show that He was one with the Father?
4. What great things has the Son of God given us?
5. Have you received what Jesus offers? Are you open to receiving more?

6

God the Holy Spirit

Let us continue observing the Trinity in creation and redemption by looking at the Holy Spirit.

The Holy Spirit testifies of Christ

In the Gospel of John, we read how Jesus introduced His disciples to the ministry of the Holy Spirit: "I will ask the Father, and he will give you another Counselor to be with you forever—the Spirit of truth" (John 14:16–17).

He goes on to say that the Holy Spirit "will teach you all things and will remind you of everything I have said to you" (John 14:26) and that "he will testify about me" (John 15:26).

This shows us that the role of the Holy Spirit is to magnify Jesus Christ to the world. Jesus made it clear all this was in the Father's plan: "He will not speak on his own; he will speak only what he hears, and he will tell you what is yet to come. He will bring glory to me by taking from what is mine and making it known to you. All that belongs to the Father is mine. That is why I said the Spirit will take from what is mine and make it known to you" (John 16:13–15).

Always remember that He is moving on hearts, achieving this even when we do not recognize Him at work. The Holy Spirit goes before us, preparing hearts to receive the testimony of Jesus and drawing people to Him as we bear witness to His life, grace, love and power.

The Holy Spirit convicts of sin

The Holy Spirit also has a ministry of convincing and convicting. Jesus prophesied, "When he comes, he will convict the

world of guilt in regard to sin and righteousness and judgment: in regard to sin, because men do not believe in me; in
regard to righteousness, because I am going to the Father,
where you can see me no longer; and in regard to judgment,
because the prince of this world now stands condemned"
(John 16:8–11).

The Spirit brings even difficult truths to bear on our hearts,
revealing eternal realities to us so that we are ready to receive
the word of Christ.

The Holy Spirit enlightens our hearts

The apostle Paul prayed fervently for believers to gain heart-
insight. He said, "I keep asking that the God of our Lord Jesus
Christ, the glorious Father, may give you the Spirit of wisdom
and revelation, so that you may know him better. I pray also
that the eyes of your heart may be enlightened in order that
you may know the hope to which he has called you, the riches
of his glorious inheritance in the saints, and his incomparably
great power for us who believe" (Ephesians 1:17–19).

This is clear evidence that the Holy Spirit desires to bring us
into a place of understanding about exactly what the Father
planned for us when He conceived of us in His mind. His
unique, creative investment in each one of us is here called
"his glorious inheritance in the saints"—contrast that with
"our inheritance" in Him (Ephesians 1:14)!

It is the Holy Spirit's reconstructive program, designed to
redirect us into the Father's will and purpose for us. He helps
us realize what Jesus paid for when He redeemed us for the
Father.

The Holy Spirit gives gifts of grace

The Father gave us creational and motivational gifts; the Son
gave us the redemptive and restorative power of salvation; but
the Holy Spirit is also a giver of gifts.

First Corinthians 12:7–11 lists nine clear "manifestations"
of the Holy Spirit, distinct from the gifts given by the Father
and the Son. These are resources for the Body that the Holy
Spirit distributes as He wills—"he gives them to each one, just

as he determines" (1 Corinthians 12:11) and as believers earnestly welcome and "eagerly desire" them (1 Corinthians 12:31; 14:1).

The purpose of these specific gifts of the Holy Spirit is to extend the graces and power of the Lord Jesus Himself through the ministry of believers. The supply of supernatural gifts enhances our work as representatives of Christ and agents of the Kingdom of God, so we can move in His life, love and power wherever we go.

Jesus gives us the gift of the Holy Spirit, yet when the Spirit comes He is loaded with packages! He desires to release much more in us and through us than we could ever imagine.

These gifts are given for delivery, not for accumulation. We receive them to pass them on to others. The power of God flows through the Body of Christ to people, both saved and lost, who need what only He can do.

Three basic categories of these spiritual gifts have been noted:

* Gifts of insight—knowledge, wisdom, discernment
* Gifts of power—faith, miracles, healing
* Gifts of—prophecy, tongues, interpretation.

In 1 Corinthians 12, Paul describes the various gifts and then goes on to compare the Church to the human body. He is showing that such a wide diversity of spiritual gifts should lead to unity, as each gift contributes something necessary for life, growth and development. Each person plays his or her part, and no one can succeed alone. There is no room for pride and arrogance, because the gifts are all freely received from our generous God. "There are different kinds of gifts, but the same Spirit. There are different kinds of service, but the same Lord. There are different kinds of working, but the same God works all of them in all men" (1 Corinthians 12:4–6). To take in the splendor of the expansive work of the Godhead—Father, Son and Spirit—brings us to a new place of amazement.

How wonderful that our Father God should have created, before all time, a plan for each one of us! How wonderful that the Son of God should have determined before all time to die to rescue sinners and see the Father's plan fulfilled! How wonderful that the Spirit of God faithfully pursues us to bring us to Christ, then equips us with resources far beyond our human capacity!

And to add to all this, by the Holy Spirit's enabling we ourselves become empowered ministers of God's life, love and power.

> Such confidence as this is ours through Christ before God. Not that we are competent in ourselves to claim anything for ourselves, but our competence comes from God. He has made us competent as ministers of a new covenant—not of the letter but of the Spirit; for the letter kills, but the Spirit gives life.
>
> 2 Corinthians 3:4–6

Study questions:

1. How does the Holy Spirit magnify both Jesus and the Father?
2. Explain the Holy Spirit's ministry of "convincing and convicting."
3. In what way does the Holy Spirit's enlightenment bring us hope?
4. What is the purpose of the gifts of the Spirit?
5. Is the Holy Spirit enabling you to move in the life, love and power of God? How can this be increasingly so in your life?

7

The Living God

The unfolding revelation of God

After the Fall of humanity broke our early close relationship with God, we lost our ability to communicate intimately with Him. Blinded human beings were far from God, wandering in sin and wallowing in bondage. But God initiated a progressive unfolding of revelation, first to reestablish fellowship (communication and relationship) and then to restore insight into His person and purpose for us.

To restore an understanding of Himself, God, like a patient teacher, began to reeducate humankind. One of the foremost ways has been by disclosing Himself through various names—terms and titles that speak of divine attributes. These names are varied not because God's nature is changeable, but because they give an ever-broadening description of His greatness, goodness and glory.

As each name was disclosed, always in life settings amid practical encounters with ready hearts, another facet of the "manifold wisdom of God" (Ephesians 3:10) was seen. *Manifold* means the "multifaceted or multicolored" glory of God, offering us an ever-enlarging picture of what God is really like.

Separation from God plunges human beings into spiritual darkness, but God has graciously poured out His life toward us: "For God, who said, 'Let light shine out of darkness,' made his light shine in our hearts to give us the light of the knowledge of the glory of God in the face of Christ" (2 Corinthians 4:6). These words speak of a dual reality: the glory of God and the face of Jesus Christ. And because it is the Holy Spirit who makes this possible, it is actually a triple reality.

In the Scriptures we see how God began step by step to reveal Himself to human beings out of touch with His glory. Season by season He disclosed attributes of His character by meeting people in circumstances where they sought or needed Him.

When He responded, often it would occasion the revealing of yet another name. This would be a term or title summarizing that very aspect of His being that shone into the darkness as divine grace invaded that human situation.

So God was progressively schooling humanity in the nature of His own fullness of being. Later, the New Testament expressed the same realities through the face of Jesus. We will compare the Hebrew and Greek names of God, and where we see Jesus revealing the light of the knowledge of God to human beings, we will realize the truth of His saying, "Whoever has seen me has seen the Father."

So let us look at fifteen names of God. We have grouped them into five main categories, which we will examine chapter by chapter:

- The living God
- The unchanging God
- The almighty God
- The saving God
- The keeping God

We will look first at how these names appear in the Old Testament, when the Creator-Father God acted in human affairs and said, "You may know me by this name." Then we will see how these names were gloriously incarnated by Jesus when He took on the nature of a human being as *Immanuel*, "God with us." In each case we will see how the Holy Spirit made this possible in Jesus' ministry and how the Spirit enables us to testify of and realize these aspects of God's character.

Jehovah, "I am"

Moses said to God, "Suppose I go to the Israelites and say to them, 'The God of your fathers has sent me to you,' and they ask me, 'What is his name?' Then what shall I tell them?"

God said to Moses, "I AM WHO I AM. This is what you are to say to the Israelites: 'I AM has sent me to you.'"

Exodus 3:13–14

Both earlier and later passages of Scripture show that God's primary and preferred name is *Yahweh (Jehovah)*. This seldom spoken name was held in deep reverence as "the Name" and reverently acknowledged as beyond definition, as ultimately God is.

But here, in God's awesome words to Moses, we are given perhaps the closest and clearest explanation of what the idea *Jehovah* means. "I AM WHO I AM"—the one who is self-existent, beyond time and space, yet ever available and present to us.

During His life on earth, Jesus unhesitatingly claimed the unique name of God for Himself. John reports this dramatic moment:

> Jesus replied, "If I glorify myself, my glory means nothing. My Father, whom you claim as your God, is the one who glorifies me. Though you do not know him, I know him.... Your father Abraham rejoiced at the thought of seeing my day; he saw it and was glad."
>
> "You are not yet fifty years old," the Jews said to him, "and yet you have seen Abraham!"
>
> "I tell you the truth," Jesus answered, "before Abraham was born, *I am!*"
>
> John 8:54–58 (emphasis added)

Jesus was not only asserting His divinity, He was specifically laying claim to that name—*Yahweh, Jehovah,* "I am that I am"—and applying it to Himself. The religious authorities understood very well what He was saying and were infuriated and attempted to execute Jesus for blasphemy.

Let us allow this passage and truth to sink deeply into our ears and hearts. There have always been those who say, "Jesus never claimed to be God—He only claimed to be an expression of God!" But here, locked in the written Word is what the incarnate Word said of Himself. Jesus stated very clearly in this text and others, that He is, literally and personally, "the self-existent One."

As God the Son, He came from beyond this world into it, so that human beings could know God and eventually be brought beyond this world to Him. Through the Holy Spirit, John heard Jesus say, "I am the Alpha and the Omega, the First and the Last, the Beginning and the End" (Revelation 22:13). And through the Holy Spirit we too can glimpse this great mystery.

Avi, Father

> Yet, O LORD, you are our Father.
> We are the clay, you are the potter;
> we are all the work of your hand.
>
> Isaiah 64:8

Avi is the Hebrew word for "father." It is the equivalent of the Aramaic word *Abba* that most people are familiar with. This name reveals the Father heart of God, also in the setting of Israel's wilderness travel (see verses 7–13). Isaiah recognizes the paternal patience that embraced them, even beyond the self-inflicted judgment that punished them.

We see this also in Moses' song, "Is he not your Father, your Creator, who made you and formed you?" (Deuteronomy 32:6).

When Jesus came to earth, first as a tiny infant, then as a boy and a grown man, He showed us the Father, in His perfect relationship to His heavenly Father. He said, "I do nothing on my own but speak just what the Father has taught me. The one who sent me is with me; he has not left me alone, for I always do what pleases him" (John 8:28–29).

Jesus revealed the Father in His very being. He said to the Pharisees, "If you knew me, you would know my Father also" (John 8:19), and at the Feast of Dedication told the Jews, "I and the Father are one" (John 10:30).

When Philip said to Jesus, "Lord, show us the Father" (John 14:8), Jesus replied, "It is the Father, living in me, who is doing his work. Believe me when I say that I am in the Father and the Father is in me; or at least believe on the evidence of the miracles themselves" (John 14:10–11).

Isaiah's amazing prophecy shows that the Son will also become a Father: "For to us a child is born, to us a son is given. . . . And he will be called . . . Everlasting Father" (Isaiah

9:6). So Jesus Himself is called the Everlasting Father of us all, joining us once more to our Creator Father God.

The Holy Spirit's work is vital in this. Paul says, "Those who are led by the Spirit of God are sons of God. For you did not receive a spirit that makes you a slave again to fear, but you received the Spirit of sonship. And by him we cry '*Abba,* Father.' The Spirit himself testifies with our spirit that we are God's children" (Romans 8:14–16).

Study questions:

1. Explain how the different names of God help to reflect the "manifold wisdom" of God.
2. In what way were circumstances of human need occasions for God to reveal different aspects of Himself?
3. What do the "I am" statements of Jesus have to do with the name *Yahweh?*
4. How does the Son reveal the Father? What part does the Holy Spirit play in this?
5. Do you know God as the great "I am" and also as loving Father?

8

The Unchanging God

Jehovah Ha Tsur, the Rock

He is the Rock, his works are perfect,
and all his ways are just.
A faithful God who does no wrong,
upright and just is he.

Deuteronomy 32:4

Deuteronomy 32 is a prophetic song of Moses, warning Israel
of the tendency of the flesh to vacillate, to change and to lack
sturdy commitment. As Moses speaks of God's covenant with
Israel, he emphasizes God's steadfastness and changelessness,
with a great rock as the picture of God's stability and firmness
of character. In this context God is called our Rock five times,
revealing His immutability—His changelessness, steadfastness
and absolute and utter reliability (verses 4, 15, 18, 30, 31).

In Psalm 95:1, God is called "the Rock of our salvation."
Jesus exactly reveals that same character, as we see in the
following verses.

In 1 Corinthians 3:11, the apostle Paul shows that Christ is
the foundation for all life: "For no one can lay any foundation
other than the one already laid, which is Jesus Christ."

The Greek term *themelion,* also used in Homer, refers to the
bedrock on which a house is built—thus the foundation upon
which you can build a life. Similarly, in Matthew 7:24–27,
Jesus refers to His teaching, including His self-designation as
"Lord" (see verses 21–22) as "the rock" upon which the wise
build their lives.

In Matthew 16:16–18, Jesus responds to Peter's declaration,

"You are the Christ, the Son of the living God," by saying that this truth was revealed "by my Father in heaven." He then adds, "On this rock I will build my church," prophesying that the Church would be founded upon Him, the Rock (Greek *petra*, a great or massive rock, contrasted with Peter's name, *Petros*, a piece of rock).

This was clearly Peter's own understanding, that upon Christ the Church is built up out of many smaller "living stones," *lithoi zoontes*, that have received of Jesus' rock-like nature.

As you come to him, the living Stone—rejected by men but chosen by God and precious to him—you also, like living stones, are being built into a spiritual house to be a holy priesthood, offering spiritual sacrifices acceptable to God through Jesus Christ. For in Scripture it says:

"See, I lay a stone in Zion,
    a chosen and precious cornerstone,
and the one who trusts in him
    will never be put to shame.

1 Peter 2:4–6

Notice that we are being built into a spiritual house, to offer spiritual sacrifices. It is through the Holy Spirit that God fulfills this promise.

El Olam, the Eternal

Lord, you have been our dwelling place
    throughout all generations.
Before the mountains were born
    or you brought forth the earth and the world,
    from everlasting to everlasting you are God. . . .
For a thousand years in your sight
    are like a day that has just gone by,
    or like a watch in the night.

Psalm 90:1–2, 4

Psalm 90 speaks of human frailty and transience of human life, but in strong contrast we see the eternal nature of God. This psalm, attributed to Moses, notes our human finiteness and fragility, especially as manifest in the deaths of those who perished in the wilderness journey. Yet God is revealed as timeless and enduring, the person who has forever been and will always be.

In John 6:40 we see Jesus laying claim to this aspect of God's nature: "For my Father's will is that everyone who looks to the Son and believes in him shall have eternal life, and I will raise him up at the last day." Jesus does not simply declare that God is eternal. He says that He has come to give us eternity! We were made for this: The preacher in Ecclesiastes says that God has "set eternity in the hearts of men" (Ecclesiastes 3:11).

Jesus told the woman at the well, "Whoever drinks the water I give him will never thirst. Indeed, the water I give him will become in him a spring of water welling up to eternal life" (John 4:14).

This cannot happen without the work of the Holy Spirit, as it is through Him that we are born again to everlasting life. In Galatians 6:8 we read, "The one who sows to please the Spirit, from the Spirit will reap eternal life."

Jehovah Shammah, The Lord is there

Among the Hebrew compound names of Jehovah, *Jehovah Shammah*—"God is present"—was introduced by Ezekiel as he prophesied hope to a demoralized remnant exiled in Babylon. God was speaking into His people's despair at being separated from the holy city, Jerusalem. He not only revealed His presence in the prophet's message, but promised a future visitation to the temple they had seen destroyed: "And the name of the city from that time on will be: THE LORD IS THERE" (Ezekiel 48:35).

This name reveals God's omnipresence—His ever-present existence in the world.

▶ The Present One

Jesus, the Son of God, came as *Emmanuel,* "God is with us." He shows us that He is faithful and tenderly says, "Surely I am with you always, to the very end of the age" (Matthew 28:20). He is truly the Present One.

Our Lord claims to be the omnipresent God—the God who is there! It is a word for us all whenever, as with those in captivity, we feel alone, distant and unsure if God is present with us anymore. Jesus told the disciples, "I will ask the Father, and he will give you another Counselor to be with you forever" (John 14:16). Through the Holy Spirit, our Comforter, Jesus says, "I'm here!"

Study questions:

1. What does the name "Rock" tell us about the character of God, and how is this reflected in Jesus?
2. In what way is the Church to express this aspect of God's nature?
3. How does Psalm 90 contrast the nature of God with that of human life?
4. Explain how the Holy Spirit manifests the Lord's omnipresence to us.
5. What does it mean to you personally that God is unchanging?

9

The Almighty God

Explaining the sovereignty of God to those who doubt

When we assert God's status as the Most High, Sovereign over all things, it is not uncommon to face human accusations: "If God really is all powerful and all loving, why does evil succeed? Either He is not all-powerful and cannot stop evil, or He is not all-loving and does not care."

It is important that believers always are "prepared to give an answer to everyone who asks you to give the reason for the hope that you have" (1 Peter 3:15). When God's sovereignty is sincerely (though ignorantly) questioned, remember:

- Our all-powerful God created all things, including our small planet.
- He created human beings to learn His ways and entrusted to them the rule of this earth and its affairs.
- This means that God's rule, by His sovereign choice, only functions on earth as human beings are obedient to God.
- Because people are disobedient and sinful, and since the time of Adam have allowed the evil one to usurp their role, they have not been able to rule rightly over the earth.
- Jesus came as the second Adam to reestablish the rule of the sovereign God and to break the power of evil whenever believers learn to live, serve and pray for His Kingdom to come.
- Each redeemed human being has been entrusted with the "keys of the kingdom of heaven" (Matthew 16:19) and has been charged to drive back the darkness of evil so that

there is a renewal of God's reign in human hearts and experience.

- In the meantime, a world hell-bent on its own will and way will inevitably grieve the Holy Spirit and continue to reap the fruit of its folly.
- When bad things happen as the result of a broken world, fallen human beings or the deliberate evil of the devil, God is blamed, doubted or cursed, not because He lacks sovereign power but because that power is not welcomed. Blinded people reject their own responsibility for evil and argue against God instead of turning to Him so that they might be saved.
- Although He is now patiently granting time for people to repent and come to Him, God intends, through Jesus' second coming, to fully reveal His sovereign power and defeat evil forever.

El Shaddai, the Almighty

When Abram was ninety-nine years old, the Lord appeared to him and said, "I am God Almighty; walk before me and be blameless."

Genesis 17:1

In Genesis 17, God revealed Himself to Abraham as *El Shaddai,* "the almighty God." God had already made a covenant with Abraham (Genesis 15), promising him that a son coming from his own body would be his heir. He had told Abraham that he would be very fruitful and that his descendants would include nations and kings. The only way that this could take place was through God's miraculous intervention, showing that all things are under His control and dominion.

Because Abraham's wife, Sarah, was infertile, they attempted to produce an heir through her maid, Hagar. But when Abraham tried to convince God to accept this son, Ishmael, as fulfillment of the promise (Genesis 17:18), God showed that He was able to do the miraculous. He revealed Himself as the all-powerful one, for whom nothing is impossible.

The name *El Shaddai* reveals God's omnipotence—He can do anything! This is paralleled in Jesus' claim, "All authority in heaven and on earth has been given to me" (Matthew 28:18). His mightiness was declared to be universal in scope. As God among us, Jesus was effectively saying, "You are looking at *El Shaddai*. The one who is omnipresent is also omnipotent."

It was through the Holy Spirit that Jesus demonstrated the power given to Him by God. He said at the very outset of His earthly ministry that "the Spirit of the Lord is on me" (Luke 4:18) to enable Him to do every great work. Jesus told the disciples, "You will receive power when the Holy Spirit comes on you" (Acts 1:8), and in the same way we manifest this power today through the Spirit's anointing.

El Elyon, God Most High

Then Melchizedek king of Salem brought out bread and wine. He was priest of God Most High, and he blessed Abram, saying,

"Blessed be Abram by God Most High,
 Creator of heaven and earth.
And blessed be God Most High,
 who delivered your enemies into your hand."
Genesis 14:18–20

This name reveals God's exalted place of dominion, and His omniscience—seeing and knowing all things from His place on high, as the Most High. The setting was Abraham's rescue of his relatives, taken hostage by foreign kings. Melchizedek directed worship as Abraham tithed the plunder he gathered.

As priest of the Most High, Melchizedek blessed Abraham, representing a spiritual continuum of worship by the faithful ones from the time of Adam. The name *El Elyon* indicates that it is the same God who is worshiped, the original Creator God who is above all. He rules over all beings as the sovereign God.

Jesus came to reintroduce the Kingdom—the sovereign rule of the Most High—to our human experience. He holds "the keys of death and Hades" (Revelation 1:18), and when He comes again it will be with the name of "KING OF KINGS AND LORD OF LORDS" (Revelation 19:16).

Then the world's kingdom will "become the kingdom of our Lord and of his Christ, and he will reign for ever and ever"

(Revelation 11:15), and the great multitude will shout, "Hallelujah! For our Lord God Almighty reigns" (Revelation 19:6). And astounding as it is, we the redeemed will be invited to rule together with Him (Revelation 5:9–10). It is all because of Jesus, the one who has come as God Most High!

The verses we have quoted here, so full of awe and worship, all come from the Revelation to John when he was "in the Spirit" (Revelation 1:10). It is the Spirit who reveals to us the unfathomable might and sovereignty of our most high God, and in turn He empowers us to share it with others.

Jehovah Sabaoth, LORD of Hosts

> Who is this King of glory? The LORD strong and mighty, the LORD mighty in battle ... The LORD of hosts, he is the King of glory.
>
> Psalm 24:8, 10, KJV

In this psalm that prophesies of a King yet to come, David uses the name of God that reveals His position as ruler of the angelic hosts, all the fearsome armies of heaven. The many Old Testament stories of God's miraculous deliverance of His people in battle confirm that He is indeed the "LORD of hosts."

► **King of the angels**

The Hebrew name *Jehovah Sabaoth,* which we read as "The LORD Almighty" in the NIV, can also be translated "LORD of Hosts," or literally, "King of the angels." That means that God's sovereign rule extends over the entire angelic realm. "The LORD Almighty—he is the King of glory," says Psalm 24:10.

The first chapter of Hebrews reveals that Jesus is also above the angelic realm, just as His Father is. It notes that after He completed His work on the cross, Jesus sat down at the right hand of the Father, having become "as much superior to the angels as the name he has inherited is superior to theirs" (Hebrews 1:4).

We know that Jesus, as the preexistent Son of God, created the angels. But this verse means that when Jesus became flesh, He walked the pathway of a perfect man who transcended even the excellence of unfallen angels. And when He comes again, He will have all the armies of heaven at His disposal to conquer the evil one, in the power of the Holy Spirit.

Adonai Jehovah, Sovereign LORD

> Abram said, "O Sovereign LORD, what can you give me?"
>
> Genesis 15:2

Abraham understood the fact that his life was under covenant commitment to God. By saying "Sovereign LORD," he acknowledged his own submissive, servant role in relationship to his owner and master. He recognized the God of his life, all his potential and his destiny.

▶ **He is Lord!**

The name *Adonai Jehovah,* "Sovereign LORD," speaks of God's position as owner or master of all. Philippians 2:9–11 affirms that Jesus also takes this title of Lord. Because He lived the life of a servant and was obedient even to death on a cross, "therefore God exalted him to the highest place and gave him the name that is above every name, that at the name of Jesus every knee should bow, in heaven and on earth and under the earth, and every tongue confess that Jesus Christ is Lord, to the glory of God the Father." Paul shows that the Holy Spirit is essential in this process of recognition and confession: "Therefore I tell you that no one who is speaking by the Spirit of God says, 'Jesus be cursed,' and no one can say, 'Jesus is Lord,' except by the Holy Spirit" (1 Corinthians 12:3).

In Mark 2 we see Jesus being attacked by the Pharisees because He confronted them with the reality of God, whom they knew only in theory. Like some today, they claimed to speak for God but refused to let Him fill their lives. Although they seemed to know the Word inside out, they did not allow it to enter from the outside in. They projected a distorted image of God, merciless and loveless and so concerned with religious rules and regulations that there was no room for humanity.

The Pharisees' claim that Jesus violated the Sabbath was born of hyper-religious sabbatical requirements, which made the day intended for rest, worship and renewal into one of fear, legal nit-picking and discomfort. Their burdensome list of humanly contrived laws disregarded the Father's intentions for the Sabbath as a day planned and set aside for human benefit (Mark 2:27).

The Pharisees had lost touch with the God who cared for people and lost touch with their own capacity to care as well. But Jesus, facing down their anger, claimed His place as "Lord even of the Sabbath" (Mark 2:28), thereby announcing Himself as God's representative. He is Lord of everything!

Study questions:

1. Can you explain to others how God is both all-powerful and all-loving?
2. How does it affect our faith to know that God is almighty?
3. In what way does Jesus show that He is the Most High God?
4. Explain the Holy Spirit's role in the declaration of Jesus as Lord.
5. Do you know God as almighty in all areas of your life?

10

The Saving God

Jehovah Tsidkenu, the Lord Our Righteousness

"The days are coming," declares the LORD,
"when I will raise up to David a righteous Branch,
a King who will reign wisely
and do what is just and right in the land.
In his days Judah will be saved
and Israel will live in safety.
This is the name by which he will be called:
The LORD Our Righteousness."

Jeremiah 23:5–6

Jeremiah prophesied powerfully of the future day when God's Messiah will execute judgment and justice in the earth. Mighty yet merciful, holy yet humble, powerful yet patient, the Lord is our Righteousness.

As the "branch," a title of the Messiah, Jesus particularly expresses the Father's nature in His role as Savior and Keeper. He came to show true righteousness to us, but also by dying for us, making it possible for us to be righteous too.

Paul declared in 1 Corinthians 1:30, "It is because of him that you are in Christ Jesus, who has become for us wisdom from God—that is, our righteousness, holiness and redemption." Jesus was not only a pure atoning sacrifice for our sins. His righteousness brings justification for us before the Father, allowing Him to rescind the record of our sin, replacing it with His own perfectly righteous record (Romans 4:5–8).

To be justified means that I can be accepted by God "just-as-if-I'd" never sinned at all! Jesus saved us despite our weakness, sin and unworthiness (Romans 5:6–11). "God made him who had no sin to be sin for us, so that in him we might become the righteousness of God" (2 Corinthians 5:21).

John says that "if our hearts do not condemn us, we have confidence before God" (1 John 3:21). He tells the Church that believers do what is right, just as Jesus is righteous, because they have been born of God (1 John 3:7, 9), and this new birth is the act of the Holy Spirit.

Jehovah Rapha, the LORD who heals

> The LORD made a decree and a law for them.... He said, "If you listen carefully to the voice of the LORD your God and do what is right in his eyes, if you pay attention to his commands and keep all his decrees, I will not bring on you any of the diseases I brought on the Egyptians, for I am the LORD, who heals you."
>
> Exodus 15:25–26

After the Israelites' escape through the Red Sea, they traveled in the desert without finding water, and after three days they came to the waters of Marah, which were so bitter that they were undrinkable. The Lord answered Moses' cry by showing him a piece of wood to throw into the water so that it supernaturally became sweet. Not only did He heal the water, but He then led them to Elim, where there were twelve springs and seventy palm trees, and there they were able to find rest.

So in this setting, God revealed His nature as the healing God. Instead of what they knew of sickness and affliction in Egypt, the Israelites could take hold of His healing power, as long as they closely obeyed Him.

One of the most notable aspects of Jesus' ministry was healing. Many healings are listed in the Gospels, and some passages indicate that countless other miraculous incidents occurred. Matthew 8:16–17 reveals that the healing ministry of Jesus directly fulfilled the prophecy of Isaiah 53:4: "Surely he took up our infirmities and carried our sorrows."

Our faith rises as we study Isaiah's prophecies of the coming healer and the Gospel reports of the fulfillment of the prophecy. Peter applies this promise to the living Church, "by his wounds you have been healed" (1 Peter 2:24). This three-fold cord of Scripture shows us that divine healing is available today as our faith may appropriate it. Jesus, like the Father, is *Jehovah Rapha*, the Lord our healer, and through the Holy Spirit we both receive and exercise healing gifts.

Jehovah Nissi, the Lord is my Banner

Moses built an altar and called it The LORD is my Banner. He said, "For hands were lifted up to the throne of the LORD."

Exodus 17:15–16

As the Israelites continued to travel through the desert, they were attacked by the Amalekites. The attack could have ended any hopes of a future free from enslavement. Moses stood on top of the hill with the staff of God in his hands. With the help of Aaron and Hur, his hands were raised up steadily until sunset so that the Amalekite army was defeated.

The picture of Moses' hands uplifted on the mountain as the battle raged in the valley shows how he was in touch with the one whose banner was raised in the invisible realm, scattering the powers of the enemy. The name of "the LORD is my Banner" rises from this event as a reminder that He causes us to triumph when we face adversity by calling out His name in prayer.

The Old Testament tells us how God led the Israelites in various battles and, as their banner, was able to bring them victory. The New Testament shows that Jesus defeated the hosts of hell in the most immense of all spiritual battles, showing Himself the victor. "Having disarmed the powers and authorities, he made a public spectacle of them, triumphing over them by the cross" (Colossians 2:15).

Paul wrote, "Thanks be to God, who always leads us in triumphal procession in Christ" (2 Corinthians 2:14). Jesus now makes victory available to us in all the issues of our daily lives and spiritual warfare, using all the resources of the Holy Spirit. He continues to save us, and we can live in that victory!

We are more than conquerors through him who loved us.

Romans 8:37

Study questions:

1. How did Jesus both show God's righteousness and also enable us to be God's righteousness?

2. Explain how God promised health to His chosen people. What were the conditions?

3. How did Jesus show that God is still our Healer? How is the Holy Spirit involved in this?

4. What does the story of Moses' uplifted hands tell us knowing God as our banner in times of spiritual battle?

5. Have you experienced God's saving power? Are you living as "more than a conqueror"?

11

The Keeping God

Jehovah Jireh, The LORD Will Provide

Abraham looked up and there in a thicket he saw a ram caught by its horns. He went over and took the ram and sacrificed it as a burnt offering instead of his son. So Abraham called that place The LORD Will Provide. And to this day it is said, "On the mountain of the LORD it will be provided."

Genesis 22:13–14

Unquestionably, one of the high points of the Old Testament is the setting revealing the Lord as our provider. Nearly forty years into his walk with God, Abraham was brought to a place of trust and surrender, as well as insight and understanding.

In his willingness to obey God, even to the point of sacrificing Isaac, Abraham showed his faith in God's faithfulness. Yet he also saw prophetically into the future, to the provision of another sacrifice, God's provision of His only Son as a substitute for humanity. He recognized the Lord as the source both of creation and redemption.

Jesus said, "Your father Abraham rejoiced at the thought of seeing my day; he saw it and was glad" (John 8:56). The faithful provider for human need is also the ultimate provider of salvation.

We commonly see God's provision in reference to physical or material need. He *is* such a provider, but the flow of material provision is rooted in the promise of salvation. The substitute of the ram for Isaac is a picture of Christ dying in our place.

In the Gospels, Jesus' feeding of the multitudes confirms His concern for ordinary human needs (John 6:1–13). But it is

58

significant that this takes place near the time of the Jewish Passover feast (verse 4). The message that follows, to do with His body and blood, reveals eternal provision for our desperate spiritual need of forgiveness and salvation (John 6:26–58).

Jesus says that just as the Father provided manna from heaven for their ancestors, "It is my Father who gives you the true bread from heaven. For the bread of God is he who comes down from heaven and gives life to the world" (John 6:32–33).

We are wise to prioritize our spiritual need when coming to God, but we need not fear requesting His provision in other ways: physical or material, economic or vocational. We should never intellectualize Christ's provision, confining it to the realm of spiritual salvation only. Philippians 4:19 spreads the table wide and invites us to expect heaven's supply at any and every point of need: "And my God will meet all your needs according to his glorious riches in Christ Jesus."

Never forget that because of what Christ has done for us on the cross, He is the channel by which God's saving power is poured out into the midst of our humanity and by which all sufficiency flows. And this provision happens through the enabling of the Holy Spirit.

Jehovah Raah, our Shepherd

The LORD is my shepherd, I shall not be in want.
He makes me lie down in green pastures,
he leads me beside quiet waters,
he restores my soul.
He guides me in paths of righteousness
for his name's sake.
Even though I walk
through the valley of the shadow of death,
I will fear no evil,
for you are with me,
your rod and your staff,
they comfort me.

Psalm 23:1–4

Our Lord is the Good Shepherd, leading, protecting, feeding, upholding. David's intimate knowledge of the shepherding task makes this tender psalm all the more significant. God is entirely skilled at the demanding task of bringing His flock to the fullest, highest and best for them. This great pastoral psalm portrays the Lord as the shepherd watching over His sheep, concerned for their well-being, gently guiding, directing and protecting.

Hebrews 13:20 speaks of Jesus as the "great Shepherd of the sheep." In John 10:1–20 Jesus speaks of Himself as the incarnation of the good shepherd, going a step further than Psalm 23 by prophesying of giving up His own life for the sake of His sheep: "I am the good shepherd; I know my sheep and my sheep know me—just as the Father knows me and I know the Father—and I lay down my life for the sheep" (John 10:14–15).

Peter addressed the elders of the early Church, charging them to care for the people as Jesus did, remembering that He will one day return: "Be shepherds of God's flock that is under your care, serving as overseers—not because you must, but because you are willing, as God wants you to be; not greedy for money, but eager to serve; not lording it over those entrusted to you, but being examples to the flock. And when the Chief Shepherd appears, you will receive the crown of glory that will never fade away" (1 Peter 5:2–4).

The qualities of love, kindness, goodness, faithfulness, gentleness and self-control that we need in this ministry are all "fruit of the Spirit" (Galatians 5:22).

Jehovah Shalom, **the Lord is Peace**

> But the Lord said to him, "Peace! Do not be afraid. You are not going to die."
> So Gideon built an altar to the Lord there and called it The Lord is Peace.
>
> Judges 6:23–24

When an angel of the Lord appeared to Gideon in response to his offering and request for a sign, he was awestruck and fearful. In an era during which darkness prevailed in many minds, many held a view of God that resembled the Canaanite deities with their vindictive anger and raw, self-serving power.

Believing that he would die for having seen God, Gideon was amazed to instead find his life purpose beginning, not ending.

Gideon's new understanding of the Lord as *Shalom,* our Peace, created a foundation for his new role as judge deliverer for Israel. Through this face-to-face encounter, he was ushered into a place of confidence in God's gracious embrace.

▶ **Our Peace**

As the Prince of Peace forecast in Isaiah 9:6, Jesus brings us peace with God and peace between all people who welcome Him. Paul put it this way in Ephesians 2:14–18: "For he himself is our peace, who has made the two one and has destroyed the barrier, the dividing wall of hostility.... His purpose was to create in himself one new man out of the two, thus making peace, and in this one body to reconcile both of them to God through the cross.... He came and preached peace to you who were far away and peace to those who were near. For through him we both have access to the Father by one Spirit." Notice that this peace works through the Holy Spirit! And Jesus causes His reconciling grace to work through us so that we too can be instruments of His peace.

In all these "named" encounters, God has revealed Himself as the God above all gods, the one like no other. He is the one who calls us to know Him and to build a life on our knowledge of who He really is.

> There is one body and one Spirit—just as you were called to one hope when you were called—one Lord, one faith, one baptism; one God and Father of all, who is over all and through all and in all.
>
> Ephesians 4:4–6

Study questions:

1. What did Abraham's understanding of God's faithfulness have to do with his obedience?
2. How did Abraham speak prophetically about God's provision in Jesus?
3. Explain how the Lord acts as the Good Shepherd to us.

4. How did Gideon's terror in the face of God turn to peace, and how is this reflected in Jesus' reconciling work?
5. Do you have a story to tell of how God has "kept" you? Do you have confidence that He will continue to do so?

Jack Hayford is founding pastor of The Church on the Way in Van Nuys, California, and chancellor of The King's College and Seminary, an interdenominational ministry training center. He is the author of more than forty books and the host of a daily radio program and weekly television program, both of which are broadcast around the world by Living Way Ministries.